CW01671813

Verses From Northern Counties

Edited by Lynsey Hawkins

YoungWriters
First published in Great Britain in 2007 by:
Young Writers
Remus House
Coltsfoot Drive
Peterborough
PE2 9JX
Telephone: 01733 890066
Website: www.youngwriters.co.uk

All Rights Reserved

© Copyright Contributors 2006

SB ISBN 1 84602 722 5

Foreword

Young Writers was established in 1991 and has been passionately devoted to the promotion of reading and writing in children and young adults ever since. The quest continues today. Young Writers remains as committed to the nurturing of poetic and literary talent as ever.

This year's Young Writers competition has proven as vibrant and dynamic as ever and we are delighted to present a showcase of the best poetry from across the UK and in some cases overseas. Each poem has been selected from a wealth of *A Pocketful Of Rhyme* entries before ultimately being published in this, our fourteenth primary school poetry series.

Once again, we have been supremely impressed by the overall quality of the entries we have received. The imagination, energy and creativity which has gone into each young writer's entry made choosing the poems a challenging and often difficult but ultimately hugely rewarding task - the general high standard of the work submitted ensured this opportunity to bring their poetry to a larger appreciative audience.

We sincerely hope you are pleased with this final collection and that you will enjoy *A Pocketful Of Rhyme Verses From Northern Counties* for many years to come.

Contents

Woodfall Primary School, Little Neston

The Poems

Identity

My brother is like a kangaroo
Because he's always stamping his feet.

My dad is a stinky ape
Because he's got bad breath.

My mam is a pretty butterfly
Because she loves flowers.

I am like a monkey
Because I climb up trees.

Bethany Green (9)
Billingham South Primary School, Billingham

Identity

My dad is like a tiger
Because he protects me from danger.
My mum is like a flamingo
Because she is beautiful and smart.
My sister is like a red-bottomed baboon
Because she is silly and stupid.
I am like a rhino
Because I'm sometimes angry.

Daniel MacDermid (8)
Billingham South Primary School, Billingham

Identity

My mum is like a monkey
because she is crazy and always loves me.

My dad is like a crocodile
because he is always snapping at me
and when he is finishing the garden he looks green.

My nana is like a fuzzy bear
because she has warm and cuddly hugs.

I am like an ox
because I am strong and hard-working.

Kaitlin Behan (8)
Billingham South Primary School, Billingham

Love

Love is like the scent of the finest perfume
trailing behind as they stroll out of the room.
Love looks like a million butterflies in the air around you.
Love feels like the thickest feathers all over you.
Love tastes like the thickest, richest chocolate melting in your mouth.

Jade Dent (10)
Billingham South Primary School, Billingham

Dad's Hiding In The Shed

Dad's hiding in the shed.
He's made me swear
Not to tell Mum
That he's hiding in there.

She was having a lie down
With the curtains drawn.
We were playing cricket
Out on the lawn.

The scores were level
It was really tense.
Dad just hit a six
Right over the fence.

I bowled the next ball
As fast as I could.
Dad tried it again
As I knew he would.

But he missed out
And the ball struck him hard on the toe.
He cried out in pain
And, as he did so,

He let go of the bat.
It flew up in an arc
And crashed through the window
Where Mum lay in the dark.

Dad's hiding in the shed.
He's made me swear
Not to tell Mum
That he's hiding in there.

Jock Wathey
Billingham South Primary School, Billingham

Short Poems

I don't like short poems me.
Short poems are stupid.
You can tell if they're bad straight away.

I quite like short poems me.
Some short poems are good
Especially the really short ones.

I love short poems me.
They're really good.
You can tell if you like them straight away.

I hate short poems me.
They're stupid.
You won't catch me reading one, not me!

Sam Swales & James Marshall (10)
Billingham South Primary School, Billingham

Hate

Hate is as black as the midnight sky.
It tastes like mouldy ale.
It smells like rotten cheese.
It looks like blood running off a waterfall.
It sounds like thunder roaring from the sky.
It feels like dying with evil.

Rebekka Dickenson (10)
Billingham South Primary School, Billingham

The Tiger

The tiger is a diesel racing car,
You see him but in a flash he has gone,
His stripes are leaping off his back.
The whiskers on his face like strings on a guitar,
His eyes are black holes,
They are piercing into his prey,
It is a red river.

His coat is a stripy scarf, orange and black.
His fangs are daggers, if you touch
Then your finger will drop off.

He eats like a beast, he could eat you in one.
He can jump over 22 buses.
His roar can be heard for miles.

Luke Ashworth (11)
Edenfield CE School, Bury

Moon

The moon is a crystal ball, it's a shiny, peeping eye
staring through the crack of my curtains.

The stars are glowing light bulbs,
flashing on and off at each other.

The night is a fast-dancing shadow,
shimmering across the floor.

The frost is a shiny snail trail
going up and down all over the world.

The sun comes up and starts chasing the stars,
moon, night and frost away.

Billy-May Novak (10)
Edenfield CE School, Bury

The Moon

The dark night jumped over the city.
My car got covered by the dark night.
Its headlights flickering like the twinkling stars above.

Nicholas Watts (10)
Edenfield CE School, Bury

The Cursed Night

As night curses the world
With its pitch-black sheet,
And the stars shine like candles,
The moon acts like a nocturnal sun.

The night creeps bit by bit
Taking over the hemisphere of the world,
The moon uses its beams to see
What havoc the night has caused.

The night strolls along the Earth
Smirking at the disasters that he has caused
And when the sun rises he goes into hiding,
Awaiting his next disastrous appearance.

Tom Holland
Edenfield CE School, Bury

Winter

The winter is taking over the summer
And you can hear the bears talking to each other,
As they are hunting for their long, cold hibernation,
Through the crystal, snowy season.

Here comes the blizzard cutting through the land,
The hills look like mountains of ice cream as far as the eye can see,
The children of the town come back
Into their warm, comfortable homes,
Like snowmen after a long, fun snowball fight.

Down comes the snow, covering the houses like a white sheet,
The cottages shiver and the sheds try to get warmer
By cuddling into the corner of the yard.
The children of the town are ice skating
On the frozen and happy lake.

The winter is taking over the summer
And you can hear the bears talking to each other,
As they are hunting for their long, cold hibernation,
Through the crystal, snowy season.

Daniel McCluskie (10)
Edenfield CE School, Bury

The Winter Spirit

The winter spirit was mocking me
As he shimmered from window to window,
Blasting in gusts of icy wind, taking out any flame still living.

He moves over the town square breathing a silky white blanket,
The trees fall victim to his sheer cold touch,
The town's shops cannot move as the winter spirit stays,
Leaving everything immobile.

The winter spirit was mocking me
As he shimmered from window to window,
Blasting in gusts of icy wind, taking out any flame still living.

Jack Gill-Burden (10)
Edenfield CE School, Bury

The Moon

The moon is a big bright bulb,
Shining over a giant black blanket.
Glowing through every nook and cranny
The big black sky tucked me into bed.

The stars watch the two corners of the world,
While everybody sleeps.
The moon is smirking and starting his evil work,
Nobody knows.

Matthew Hoyle (11)
Edenfield CE School, Bury

Night

Night is a black hole,
He makes me feel sleepy,
His face looks like a dark bedroom,
His eyes are beautiful stars,
His mouth is dark clouds,
His hair is like shooting stars shooting past my window,
His clothes are made of black silk,
When he speaks he makes me jump,
He lives in a dark black hole with stars shooting past
And the moonlight creeping round the corner.

Ellie Richards (10)
Edenfield CE School, Bury

The Night

The night stalks the world,
Never stopping, leaving frost in his wake,
Always chasing the day but not succeeding,
He hugs the world as he extends his wrath.

He covers cities, towns and villages,
Using the moon to see where he's going,
His client is the sandman sending you to sleep,
The stars are his brothers blinking in the night.

His cold temper freezes the world,
His black heart throws a shadow across the Earth,
He sends his power through the night,
The day spreads its light to bring new life.

Josh Rimmer (11)
Edenfield CE School, Bury

The Night

The moon is a flaming light bulb,
It shouts night-night with its powerful rays.
Shine, shine, shine, that's all it does,
But there's no place for it in the day.

The stars are God's twinkling toes,
Every time they twinkle they take another stride.
They're so bright they burn my nose,
Whenever the sun comes out I try to hide.

The night wakes the Earth,
It constantly prods me in my bed.
He wants to be seen,
But when I climbed out of bed he wasn't there.

Harry Elford (10)
Edenfield CE School, Bury

Grandfather Night

The night is a pitch-black duvet
Who covers you in darkness.
The snow is shivering the leaves off with its frost.
The church clock strikes 12 midnight.
The owl of the great oak tree
Is going to search for his prey.

The sun arrives, floating to the sky.
The night is defeated by his arch-enemy.
He knows when the sun appears.
Beams run down fast as the bluebird.
The sun smiles and light covers half of the world with sunshine.
The night is destroyed.

Luke Taylor (10)
Edenfield CE School, Bury

The Moon

The moon is a giant shining diamond ball
With a candle in its hand
It wraps its arms around the villages, cities and towns

As night comes and the dark draws near
The moon enchants the world
With a circle of light, constantly watching you

When you slip open your curtain
There it is, staring at you
With its gigantic beady eyes
A strip of its light beaming
Through the gap in your room.

Joe Bibby (11)
Edenfield CE School, Bury

The Moon

The moon is a giant ping-pong ball,
Sweeping across the sky.
The stars are shining light bulbs,
Blinking through the night.
The dark night walks round the world,
Tucking me in as he passes.
The night is my pillow,
Comfy as can be.

The night is a graceful ballroom dancer,
Moving round the world.
The wind strokes the trees,
With her gentle breeze.
The night creeps round the world,
Watching what we are doing,
With his moonlight torch.

Olivia Studholme (10)
Edenfield CE School, Bury

On Hallowe'en Night

Werewolves howl, witches cackle,
Zombie footballers cannot tackle.
Monsters hide under the bed,
Out they come to eat your head.

Dracula's teeth far too sharp,
He could chew through a carp.
Baby ghouls learn to float,
They even might eat your throat.

The holiday of scare and fright,
Trick or treaters come all night.
Pumpkins light up all the street,
Ghosts and ghouls you might meet.

Melissa Marshall (10)
Golden Flatts Primary School, Hartlepool

Hallowe'en

People dressing up for Hallowe'en.
Children knocking on your door.

'Trick or treat?' they all shout,
'Oh what a night!'

People having parties in their homes,
Music loud and children dancing,
People screaming, others fighting.

Some houses decorated,
Bats, pumpkins, ghosts and witches,
Sparkling lights and other things bright.

'Hallowe'en, oh what a night!'

Amy Cook (10)
Golden Flatts Primary School, Hartlepool

The Spook's Monologue

Chocolate, chocolate ever so tasty,
Especially with a touch of pastry.
Witches like it very much,
And they add their very own touch.

A touch of frog leg, a touch of chicken,
Mix it together and the spoon is good enough for lickin'.
When you try to cast a spell,
Remember not to go to Hell!

I saw a girl dressed up as a witch,
Then I got a tiny twitch.
Hallowe'en creepy spook,
Witches always try to cook.

Don't be mean, be so keen,
Come on kids, it's Hallowe'en!

Jassem Sukar (10)
Golden Flatts Primary School, Hartlepool

Hallowe'en Poem

Vampires' toenails, witches' hair too,
And all with the help of a gorilla from the zoo.
Sweets from Hallowe'en thrown in a pot,
Mix it up well and then boil until hot.

A dancing dog and a hairy frog,
A beaver thrown in there too.
My Hallowe'en cauldron will not be complete,
Without the all important, you!

James Lees (11)
Golden Flatts Primary School, Hartlepool

Hallowe'en At Midnight

Zombies groan,
Witches moan,
Voodoo dolls,
Giant trolls.
Big rats
And mad cats,
They all like to eat you,
Make sure they don't meet you!
Mummies have empty tummies
And they are really funny.

Joseph Smith (10)
Golden Flatts Primary School, Hartlepool

Hallowe'en Poem

Vampires come out at night,
their rough mouldy skin cannot stand light.
Devils' bodies, very, very red
with those vicious horns sticking out their head.

Goblins' skin, the colour of a bogie from my nose,
green and slimy like my toes!
A witch can be scary, her legs are so hairy,
and her big black cat matches her hat.

Seeing a zombie makes me jump out my pants,
the way it walks, that freaky stance.
On that night there will be a scream
for one good reason, it's Hallowe'en!

Jamie Ingram (10)
Golden Flatts Primary School, Hartlepool

Hallowe'en

H owling horror
A lmighty aliens
L ovely lights
L icking lips
'O oting owl
W icked witch
E mpty energy
E erie echoes
N oisy night.

Cameron Boddy (10)
Golden Flatts Primary School, Hartlepool

Hallowe'en

Door creaked
Ghosts howled
Bats flew
Children screamed
Witches spelled
Wolves hunted
Children partied
Cauldrons bubbled
Pumpkins beamed
Black cats screeched
Dracula ate
Toads croaked
Ghouls scared
Bats waved

Hallowe'en, beware!

Michael Burn (10)
Golden Flatts Primary School, Hartlepool

Hallowe'en Night

There is a night called Hallowe'en
Most people get scared and give a scream
There are costumes like witches, bats and ghosts
The witches often like to roast their ghosts
Watch out though they like to mix you
Make sure they don't pick you.

When the clock strikes 12
Out come the elves from behind your shelves
That's the ghost's favourite part of the night
When they come to give you a fright.

If children come to trick or treat
Don't be greedy, give them a sweet.

Josie Naylor (10)
Golden Flatts Primary School, Hartlepool

It's Hallowe'en

Hallow, hallow, Hallowe'en,
The time where creepy spooks are seen.
Look over here, look over there,
Argh! Spooks in my underwear.

Creepy witches fly high in the night,
They just might shout boo! and give you a fright.
Skeletons crackle, their bones jumble,
Zombies moan and ghosts bumble.

The wizard's feet are very smelly,
The hairs on the werewolf are the size of my belly.
So remember hallow, hallow, Hallowe'en,
I'm really scared after the spooks I've seen.

Sophie Armstrong (10)
Golden Flatts Primary School, Hartlepool

The Life Of A Victorian Child

Sadness is the never-ending running blood on my feet,
Sadness is being in the workhouse,
Sadness is the emptiness in my tummy,
Sadness is the pitch-black soot burning in my eyes.

Daniel Longhorn (10)
Mansfield Primary School, Ellesmere Port

The Life Of A Victorian Child

Sadness is the cuts on my knees
Sadness is the soot in my throat
Sadness is the food that my family doesn't get
Sadness is the hunger in my stomach
Sadness is the cane on my hand.

Charlotte Lenton (10)
Mansfield Primary School, Ellesmere Port

The Life Of A Victorian Child

Sadness is the blood on my feet,
Sadness is the rumble of my empty stomach,
Sadness is the pitch-black soot in my eye,
Sadness is working in the workhouse,
Sadness is the coldness of the street.

Lewis Molyneux (10)
Mansfield Primary School, Ellesmere Port

Life Of A Victorian Child

Sadness is the soot on young children's chests.
Sadness is children with cuts on their feet
because they have no shoes.
Sadness is the fear of dying
when they work in the factories.
Sadness is when they get no food.
Sadness is all the jobs they have to do.
Sadness is the cane on their hand.

Zoe Wojtala (10)
Mansfield Primary School, Ellesmere Port

My Weekly Poem

Monday, a fresh start of the week.
Tuesday, it's just another day.
Wednesday, we let the day go by.
Thursday, a sparkle in my eye.
Friday, my friends are going by.
Saturday, the fun has just begun.
Sunday, the laughter and cheer will be near

And that was my weekly poem.

James O'Regan (10)
Mansfield Primary School, Ellesmere Port

Animals

Zebra, zebra, zebra
Strong, stripy, smart zebra
Zebra, zebra, zebra
Black, bright, beautiful zebra

Lion, lion, lion
Sleepy, snoring, strong lion
Lion, lion, lion
Lazy, leaping, laughing lion

Elephant, elephant, elephant
Stomping, staring, smart elephant
Elephant, elephant, elephant
Big, bossy, brave elephant.

Lauren Moss (9)
Our Lady & St Gerard's RC Primary School, Preston

Ice Cream

I cy and delicious.
C aramel, strawberry, chocolate or vanilla.
E ither/or, take your pick.

C an you get raspberry flavour?
R eally I can't choose whether to have sprinkles or not.
E very different topping please, I can't choose.
A delicious creamy mixture.
M ine at last, yum, yum, mmmmm!

Caitlin Morgan (9)
Our Lady & St Gerard's RC Primary School, Preston

Summer Sun

In the summer sun
We go out and play
It's always a lot of fun
So we dance around all day.

In the summer sun
We go to the park
We're walking down the path
And we hear dogs bark.

In the summer sun
We go to the beach
We jump up for the ball
And do a very good reach.

In the summer sun
We go to the town
We're shopping all day
And we see a funny clown.

Beth Gallery (9)
Our Lady & St Gerard's RC Primary School, Preston

Hallowe'en

Hallowe'en, Hallowe'en
Hear a shout, hear a scream
See a ghost, run wild
I'm acting like a child!

Orange pumpkin
Scary eyes
Boo! Behind you
Big surprise!

The babies always look
Ahh, very sweet
Knock on the door
Bang! 'Trick or treat!'

Elizabeth Cronin (9)
Our Lady & St Gerard's RC Primary School, Preston

Animals

A nts, small and black with no hair,
N ewts crawl in the bright sun when it's very hot,
I nsects are small and wide,
M onkeys are cute and fluffy,
A nimals are different to humans apart from gorillas,
L ions roar very loud and scary,
S lugs are very slow and love rain.

Danielle Morgan (9)
Our Lady & St Gerard's RC Primary School, Preston

Hallowe'en

The sky is dark
The moon is bright
It's a very scary night.

Children on the doorstep
Ringing the doorbell
'Trick or treat?' they say to me.

But this is what I think!

Witches looking through the window
Black cats in the backyard
And ghosts in the garden.

Kate Nowell (10)
Our Lady & St Gerard's RC Primary School, Preston

Autumn

All the leaves,
On the trees,
Are starting to fall,
And Hallowe'en is starting to call,
The children can't wait to trick or treat,
To go round and get some sweets,
Now we can go onto Bonfire Night,
And the big *'booms'* give people a fright,
Now you can go and eat some treacle toffee
And have a good old cup of coffee.

Niamh Hall (9)
Our Lady & St Gerard's RC Primary School, Preston

Shapes

C ones,
I sosceles triangles,
R ectangles and
C ylinders,
L ovely shapes, really good ones,
E ven one more, called a
S phere.

Conor Sherliker (10)
Our Lady & St Gerard's RC Primary School, Preston

Winter

Winter is windy.
Winter is fun.
Winter is wonderful.
Winter is for snowmen.
Winter is for happiness.
Winter is for Christmas
And Christmas is for fun.
Winter is snow time
And a winter wonderland.
Winter is wonderful fun.

Alex Williams (9)
Our Lady & St Gerard's RC Primary School, Preston

Nonsense Times

Oh when Old Mother Hubbard
Locked her dog in a cupboard,
And the King put sixpence in his pie,
And in Hey Diddle-Diddle
The dog broke the fiddle,
And Humpty knocked over the wall,
When the Billy Goats Gruff taught us to bluff
And old Captain Hook was a new crook,
And dear Cinderella locked her sisters in the cellar,
Was all in nonsense times
When everyone wrote rhymes.

Edward Bowman (9)
Our Lady & St Gerard's RC Primary School, Preston

My School

At school,
I don't think it's cool.
I'm in class 8,
I've never been late.
I'm in Year 5,
I like the drink Five Alive.
Yesterday I learnt how to draw a frog
And build a machine using a cog.

Lewis Mather (9)
Our Lady & St Gerard's RC Primary School, Preston

Animals

A t night the bats fly away
N ot a sound from the hunting tigers
I mpossible to see are the ants
M eat-eating lions love their meals
A t midnight the wolves howl at the moon
L emurs running from the foosa
S winging through the jungle the monkeys play.

Matthew Skellorn (10)
Our Lady & St Gerard's RC Primary School, Preston

Animals In Kenya

Tiger, tiger, tiger
Pouncing, preying, purring tiger
Tiger, tiger, tiger
Great, growling, grumpy tiger.

Tiger, tiger, tiger
Big battling, beastly tiger
Tiger, tiger, tiger
Fluffy, furry, fierce tiger.

Tiger, tiger, tiger
Dashing, dangerous, dastardly tiger
Tiger, tiger, tiger
Running, rushing, roaring tiger.

Tiger, tiger, tiger
Terrific, terrifying tiger,
Tiger, tiger, tiger
Fit, fat, fabulous tiger.

Ryan Heyworth (9)
Our Lady & St Gerard's RC Primary School, Preston

Kenyan Animals

Zebra, zebra, zebra
So stripy, so fast, so muscly
Zebra, zebra, zebra
So strong, so tall, so large.

Elephant, elephant, elephant
So heavy, so big, so grey
Elephant, elephant, elephant
So slow, so fat, so large.

Crocodile, crocodile, crocodile
So large, so green, so wild
Crocodile, crocodile, crocodile
So sharp, so strong, so big.

David Bryant (10)
Our Lady & St Gerard's RC Primary School, Preston

Animal Alphabet Poem

A lligator goes *snap, snap, snap.*
B umblebee goes *buzz, buzz, buzz.*
C at goes *miaow, miaow, miaow*
D og barks, *woof, woof, woof.*
E lephant goes *stomp, stomp, stomp.*
F ish goes *blub, blub, blub.*
G orilla goes *oooh, oooh, oooh.*
H orse goes *neigh, neigh, neigh.*
I guanas stay quiet all day.
J ackal goes *ow ow oowwwww.*
K angaroo goes *thump, thump, thump.*
L ion goes *roar, roar, roar.*
M ice go *squeak, squeak, squeak.*
N ewt goes *slither, slither, slither.*
O ctopus goes *splash, splash, splash.*
P arrot goes *squawk, squawk, squawk.*
Q uails go *tweet, tweet, tweet.*
R ats go *nibble, nibble, nibble.*
S nakes go *hiss, hiss, hiss.*
T apir goes *snort, snort, snort.*
U nicorn goes . . . no one knows.
V ulture goes *screech, screech, screech.*
W allaby goes *bounce, bounce, bounce.*
X oliazebria . . . this one's a secret.
Y aks make a mooing sound.
Z ebra goes *eee ooh eee ooh.*

Jade Ollerton (9)
Our Lady & St Gerard's RC Primary School, Preston

Hallowe'en

It's dark out there with kids all around
Witches and ghosts fly everywhere
Knock, knock on the door, 'Trick or treat?
Give me something good to eat!'
See all the pumpkins, orange and bright
Shining there for all the night!

Nicole McGrail (9)
Our Lady & St Gerard's RC Primary School, Preston

Hallowe'en Howl

The moon's out bright
The wolves all howl.

The witches on the brooms
The cats go miaow.

The pumpkins shine
The ghosts all whine.

As vampires sleep
The ghouls, they weep.

See the devils with their horns
And the bats that squeal at dawn.

It's been a scary night,
I hope it's been a *happy Hallowe'en fright!*

Alexandra Lane (9)
Our Lady & St Gerard's RC Primary School, Preston

Football

F ootball is an art
O n every week
O h, I think it is a goal
T eamwork is what you need
B eckham is classic at free kicks
A nimals can't play
L inesmen are needed
L ooking for the ball to cross the line.

Luke Walsh (9)
Our Lady & St Gerard's RC Primary School, Preston

Bad Weather

B ringing sadness to the people,
A nd splashing everywhere,
D ripping in the buckets.

W ith rain, colds are in the air,
E ntirely covered by lightning,
A nd we're begging for the sun,
T o be warm and dry, I'll want to be first one,
H ooray, it's stopped, finally,
E nter your warm bedroom,
R eady for your tea.

Hayley Kane (9)
Our Lady & St Gerard's RC Primary School, Preston

Hallowe'en

H aunted houses around every corner,
A liens lurk all around,
L ovely blood, a tasty drink,
L ights shine from pumpkins,
O wls hoot and fly all around,
W ine gums, chocolate and lollies as a treat,
E vil laughs and people everywhere,
E ven animals with vicious teeth,
N ever bump into a skeleton with . . . ?

Amy Newsham (9)
Our Lady & St Gerard's RC Primary School, Preston

Tiger, O Tiger

Tiger, O tiger you roar and roar
Tiger, O tiger you snore and snore
Tiger, O tiger you come out to play
Tiger, O tiger you walk away.

Tiger, O tiger you live in a jungle
Tiger, O tiger you sleep in a bundle
Tiger, O tiger you leap and leap
Tiger, O tiger you go fast asleep.

Caitlin Chappell (9)
Our Lady & St Gerard's RC Primary School, Preston

Friends

F riends are like gold
R eally precious even if you're old
I f you're best friends you're never apart
E ndless love when you start
N ever fall out over silly things
D oing what friends do best
S taying together forever.

Niall Wilson (9)
Our Lady & St Gerard's RC Primary School, Preston

Favourite Animals

Lion, lion, lion
Rough, roaring, running lion
Lion, lion, lion
Fast, fierce, ferocious lion

Zebra, zebra, zebra
Strong, stripy, skinny zebra
Zebra, zebra, zebra
Fit, fleeing, fantastic zebra

Giraffe, giraffe, giraffe
Long, lean, lovely giraffe
Giraffe, giraffe, giraffe
Tall, terrific, long-tongued giraffe.

Natalie Howard (9)
Our Lady & St Gerard's RC Primary School, Preston

Animals

Lion, lion, lion
Rapid, roaring, raging lion
Lion, lion, lion
Deadly, dangerous, drooling lion

Zebra, zebra, zebra
Strong, stripy, soft zebra
Zebra, zebra, zebra
Fit, fast, furious zebra

Monkey, monkey, monkey
Chatty, cheeky, chomping monkey
Monkey, monkey, monkey
Naughty, nutty, nasty monkey.

Callum Roe (9)
Our Lady & St Gerard's RC Primary School, Preston

Hallowe'en

H is for howling, that's the sound a werewolf makes
A is for apples, witches love them rotten
L is for lamps, we use them in the dark
L is for loud, that's what ghosts are
O is for owls that are noisy all night
W is for witches, look at her cat
E is for exciting, while we trick or treat all night
E is for enchanting, like a witch's book
N is for monsters never giving up chasing you.

Leanne Owen (9)
Our Lady & St Gerard's RC Primary School, Preston

Hallowe'en

There's a full moon out tonight,
And the pumpkins all shine bright,
Oh look it's my friends, they gave me a fright.

One as a cat,
The other's a bat,
Another's a pumpkin plump and fat.

Now off I go to trick or treat,
Oh I've got some sweets,
They look tasty, I can't wait till I eat.

Hallowe'en.

Madison Brown (9)
Our Lady & St Gerard's RC Primary School, Preston

The Worst Witch

The worst witch
Comes out at night

Sleepy, dizzy
Wrapped up tight.
Kids in bed
Wake up at night
To have a drink of blood

In the morning
Kids wake up
While witches settle down
Sleeping in their faraway land
Whilst yellow and light on Earth

Hallowe'en comes
Rather quick

Knock-knock
At number eight
'Trick or treat
Give me something
Sweet to eat.'

It's time for bed!

Jessica Speight (9)
Our Lady & St Gerard's RC Primary School, Preston

In The Jungle

Elephant your trunk,
A leathery skin,
Cradling the sun,
One home.

In the jungle,
The mysterious jungle.

Your ears are two dead leaves,
Folds of skin,
For fanning,
One place.

In the jungle,
The mysterious jungle.

A tail like a long thin whip,
Eyes that show your spirit,
Eyes like marbles,
One home.

In the jungle,
The mysterious jungle.

Your skin is as tough as steel,
Your call drifts round the world
To end up in
One place.

James Toulmin (10)
Ouston Junior School, Chester-le-Street

Elephant, I Saw You

In the green of the grass,
Elephant, I saw you,
Staring.

Your tusks
Like yellow umbrella handles.

In the green of the grass,
Elephant, I saw you,
Shading your skin.

Your skin as wrinkly
As a grandpa's face.

In the green of the grass,
Elephant, I saw you,
Flopping your ears.

Your ears
Like big floppy rugs.

In the green of the grass,
Elephant, I saw you,
Standing.

You were calling,
Calling to your baby.

Natasha Jackson (10)
Ouston Junior School, Chester-le-Street

The Call Of An Elephant

In the darkness of the jungle
Elephant, I heard you,
Stomping.

Your ears are giant fans.
Bigger than a lorry,
Your body stands there.

In the darkness of the jungle
Elephant, I heard you,
Trumpeting.

Your eyes like black stones,
They're a deep, dark pit of fear.

In the darkness of the jungle
Elephant, I heard you,
Calling.

Your skin is a dark grey,
It shivers for life,
It is dying with pain.

In the darkness of the jungle
Elephant, I heard you,
Crying, crying for your life.

Brandon McNeil (11)
Ouston Junior School, Chester-le-Street

The Wonderful Elephant

In the deep of the jungle,
I saw you, standing proud.

In the deep of the jungle,
I saw you, trumpeting.

In the deep of the jungle,
I saw you, stamping.

In the deep of the jungle,
I saw you, with eyes like black pebbles.

In the deep of the jungle,
I saw you, standing proud.

In the deep of the jungle,
I saw you, with skin as crumpled as creased leather.

In the deep of the jungle,
I saw you, with flapping ears.

In the deep of the jungle,
I saw you, standing proud.

Lauren Smart (10)
Ouston Junior School, Chester-le-Street

The Call Of The Elephant

In the gold sand,
Elephant,
I saw you calling.

Whipping tail,
Skinny as a washing line,
Ready to whip.

In the gold sand,
Elephant,
I saw you crying.

Shiny black eyes,
As dark as the night sky,
Watching for hunters.

In the gold sand,
Elephant,
I saw you crying.

Banana-shaped tusk,
White as chalk,
Ready to stab.

In the gold sand,
Elephant,
I saw you crying.

Long trunk,
Strong as a bear,
Ready to attack.

In the gold sand,
Elephant,
I saw you crying.

Carl Ruddick (10)
Ouston Junior School, Chester-le-Street

The Strong Elephant

In the centre of the green forest
Elephant, I saw you prowling

Rough skin like dark, rough sandpaper
Which strokes against rocks

Eyes staring eagerly
Which are as black as burnt coal

In the centre of the green forest
Elephant, I saw you stamping

Your feet so strong three of the strongest people in the world
Couldn't lift them

In the elephant's body
Its heart beating as slow as a dying old woman

In the centre of the green forest
Elephant, I saw you dying.

Daniel Bradbury (10)
Ouston Junior School, Chester-le-Street

Old People

Their hands are wrinkled and shake like leaves on a tree.
Their faces are as wrinkled and lined like mouldy raisins.
Their eyes are like shimmering sparkles.
Their clothes are smart and groovy like Elvis.
How do they move slowly
and carefully like a turtle?

Harry O'Neill (7)
Prestbury CE Primary School, Prestbury

Old People

Their hands are wrinkled and shake like leaves on a tree.
Their faces are like woodchips.
Their eyes are blue, shining in the moonlight.
Their clothes are old and red.
They move like a snail.
They are thinking of memories.
I think they are nice because they tell me stories.

Alasdair Paton (7)
Prestbury CE Primary School, Prestbury

Unknown Night

Hitting each other in the wind,
Human-like hands glimpse in the light,
Shadow casting,
Graceful figure.

Scowling on the atmosphere below,
A dazzling silver glimpse,
A round sphere of glowing snow,
Shimmering moon,
Graceful moon.

Whistling down the spooky stream,
Not a care in the world,
Silently rippling,
Cannot stop.

A ball of fur clutching two beady eyes,
Watching you from every corner,
Lurking in the shadows,
Purring relentlessly,
Hissing silently.

All is oblivious to the living!

Ellen Wilkinson (9)
Prestbury CE Primary School, Prestbury

Night Poem

Night, night is spooky, scary, creepy,
Night has ghostly trees.

Howling, wailing trees waving in the breeze,
You hear them in the night, you feel them,
The bony branches all hard and spiky.

Cats, they spy on you, silent as a mouse.
They stare with their green glowing eyes,
Like a lion waiting to pounce on its prey.

The night is alive, very alive!

Ellie Heron (9)
Prestbury CE Primary School, Prestbury

Dawn Is Approaching

Outside is full of swooping trees,
Dying leaves thumping to the ground,
Swinging trees,
Rootless trunks.

Like a glimmering disco ball in the sky,
So clear the people on it can be seen,
Shimmering stars,
Lumps up high.

Eyes glowing like green emeralds,
Cats purring and spying for prey,
Climbing suspiciously,
Silent purring.

River trickling over stones,
Moon shimmering over the water,
Splish, splash,
River flowing.
Dawn is creeping, don't be scared!

Cara Harcombe (10)
Prestbury CE Primary School, Prestbury

Night Poem

Moon so bright, simmering,
Gleaming in the light.
Floating in the air,
Silver moon is there.

The wailing trees shivering,
Is just a daily breeze.
Dying leaves,
Falling down.

Cats scratching at the door,
Eyes glowing in the dark.
Cats hissing,
Climbing viciously.

River flowing without a sound,
Bumping against the rocks.
Drifting away,
Splashing about.

Bats are squeaking loudly,
Beady eyes are flying around you.
Wings as bony as fingers,
Swooping high.

The night is alive
Dawn is now approaching.

Polly Hedley (9)
Prestbury CE Primary School, Prestbury

Night

Trees are swaying, though there is no wind,
They are watching you,
Warning you off,
Dark figures,
Always there.

The moon, a bright ball of light,
A lump of emptiness,
Snow in the sky,
An icy silver,
Watery surface.

The river drifts silently, danger in its depths,
Coming for you in the dark,
Walking in the night,
Lifeless and dark.
This starry night hides the danger.

Katherine Monaghan (9)
Prestbury CE Primary School, Prestbury

Night

Outside is full of blowing trees.
Bony branches blowing in the breeze,
Swishing trees, dying leaves.

The moon like a ball of snow,
Like a night light up above,
Reflecting in the river's a glittering moon.

Grass like a dewy wet carpet,
Sticking on your feet, lit up with the moonlight,
A dull dark green.

The river drifting by,
And galloping like horses over the little rocks,
Splashing, never stopping.
The night is alive.

Herbie Kemp (10)
Prestbury CE Primary School, Prestbury

The Dead Of Night

Trees swaying side to side,
Branches like old veiny fingers
Reaching out,
Rustling leaves,
Shadowy trees.

River, silver like a starry night,
Swooshing side to side
Like a waterfall
Hitting the rocks at the bottom,
Moon reflected,
Splashing.

Cats' eyes glowing
Like the sun in daylight,
Teeth and paws like sharp glass,
Scratching desperately,
Prowling loudly.

Moon, like a bright ball of snow,
Glistening in the air like ice,
Shining till dawn,
Silver like money.

Moon hiding, sun appears.

Rebecca Clark (9)
Prestbury CE Primary School, Prestbury

Night Is Awake

Trees, the wind makes them look like swaying ghosts,
The wind makes them howl like a pack of wolves,
Swinging trees,
Rootless trees.

Like a glittering ball in the sky,
Moon, reflecting into the lake,
Shining moon,
Silver moon.

Cats spying on you every night,
Snooping around for their prey,
Miaowing loudly,
Creeping slowly.

Alice Jones (9)
Prestbury CE Primary School, Prestbury

Night Poem

Outside is full of trees groaning like ghosts,
Trees whooshing like prowling figures,
Creeping branches,
Falling leaves.

Cats creeping around with glowing eyes,
Prowling and screeching in the garden,
Silently creeping,
Purring and crying.

The moon glistens in the night,
The moon floating in the sky like a ball of ice,
Glittering,
Glistening.

Morning's here.

Max Newcombe (9)
Prestbury CE Primary School, Prestbury

Elephant

Flapping ears in the beautiful night
Swinging its trunk to and fro
Plodding slowly through the jungle
Charging fast through the wet rainforest
Big, bulgy elephant charging through the coconut trees
Stomping fast through the warm, splashing water.

Scott Woolley (7)
Prestbury CE Primary School, Prestbury

Night Poem

Outside is full of swaying trees,
Branches waving in the breeze,
Dying leaves,
Trees blowing.

The moon, a ball of shiny white,
Brightly flashing out the light,
Glistening,
A scary shape.

River flowing silently,
Overgrown banking at the edge,
Splashing,
A dark colour.

Dawn is rising!

Georgia Burgess (9)
Prestbury CE Primary School, Prestbury

Night Is Alive

Outside is full of ghostly trees,
Thumping each other in the gloomy night,
Whispering secrets,
Hushed.

The moon is a lump of ice in the sky,
Silver swaying moon,
Shimmering,
Reflection.

Trickling over tumbling stones,
The current swirling like a whirlpool,
Clear,
Splashing.

Cats spy mischievously,
Creeping low to the ground,
Eyes sparkling,
Green as grass.

Night is alive!

Chloe Marshall (9)
Prestbury CE Primary School, Prestbury

Night

Outside in the darkness the trees are blowing,
Shadows are coming and a creepy breeze,
Trees upon you,
Once again.

The moonlight is broken, shining down,
On the river gazing back up,
A gazing light,
Golden moon.

Cats watching you from every corner,
Looking at you with creepy, beady eyes,
Lurking cats,
Creepy cats.

Whistling down the spooky stream,
Spooky waves drifting up behind you,
Water rippling,
Water flowing.

The light is coming.

Max Pemberton (9)
Prestbury CE Primary School, Prestbury

The Night Is Alive

Trees rustling in the wind,
Shadows casting, something might jump,
Trunks creaking,
They are pitch-black.

Cats have beady eyes that watch your every move,
Creeping round corners, following you,
Silent but deadly,
You'd better watch out.

Foxes are very cunning and spiteful,
They hunt down their prey like a tiger searching for its dinner,
They are very fast,
Swishing tails.

Rivers slowly creep over rocks,
There is a drip, drop,
They are rapid,
They bubble.

Owls hooting to each other,
Searching for mice and rats,
They have glowing eyes,
Twitching heads.

Badgers are fierce like a cat,
They're silent like a shark,
They scamper across the floor,
Like mice.
The night is alive!

Rebecca O'Brien (9)
Prestbury CE Primary School, Prestbury

Night Poem

Outside is full of screeching trees,
Wailing and moving in the wind,
Bony branches,
Creeping silently.

Lumps of ice roaming in the sky,
A big ball of light,
Gleaming unnoticed,
A silver effect.

A fierce, fuzzy machine that never stops,
Claws as sharp as sharks' teeth,
Beady eyes,
Purring loudly.

Flowing silently, drifting light,
Creeping closer and closer,
Reflection of the silver moon
But you don't know that they're there.

Freya Rottenbury (9)
Prestbury CE Primary School, Prestbury

Old People

Their hands are wrinkly and lined like raisins.
Their faces are bright and sparkly like the stars in the sky.
Their eyes are bright like the sun sparkling.
Their clothes are smart and colourful like a rainbow.
How do they move? Slow but can go fast sometimes.
What are they thinking, good memories?
What do you think about them, nice people?

Gabrielle Rayner (7)
Prestbury CE Primary School, Prestbury

Elephant

Big, bulgy elephant charging through the coconut trees.
Plodding slowly through the hot jungle.
Charging fast through the wet rainforest.
Stamping around the sandy path.

Daisy Rowley (7)
Prestbury CE Primary School, Prestbury

Old People

Their hands are wrinkled and shake, like leaves on a tree.
Their faces are wrinkly and lined like raisins.
Their eyes are bright and sparkly like the shimmering stars
in the night sky.
Their clothes are smart and colourful like a rainbow.
How do they move? They run as fast as a spotty cheetah.
What are they thinking of, lovely memories?
What do you think? I love old people.

Ella Seaborn (8)
Prestbury CE Primary School, Prestbury

Old People

Their hands are wrinkled and shake like leaves on a tree.
Their faces are crinkled like a paper bag.
Their eyes are sparkly like stars.
Their clothes are colourful like rainbows.
They move slowly.
They think of good stories.
The best thing about them is they are funny.

Hannah Lithgow (7)
Prestbury CE Primary School, Prestbury

Elephant

Big, bulgy elephant charging through the coconut trees.
Plodding slowly through the hot jungle.
Charging fast through the wet rainforest.
Large flying trunk splashing in the cool water.
Big ears flapping.
Beware!
Tail flapping.

Matthew Gardner (7)
Prestbury CE Primary School, Prestbury

Elephant

Big, bulgy elephant charging through the coconut trees.
Stamping around the sandy path.
Stomping fast through the warm splashing water.
Strolling peacefully in the boiling sunshine.
Charging through the wet rainforest.
Swishing its trunk to and fro.
Flapping ears in the twilight.
Slapping tail flicking all night.

Teigan Busby (7)
Prestbury CE Primary School, Prestbury

Elephant

Big, bulgy elephant charging through the coconut trees.
Stamping around the sandy path.
Stomping fast through the warm splashing water.
Strolling peacefully in the boiling sunshine.
Charging fast through the wet rainforest.
Swishing its trunk to and fro.
Flapping ears in the twilight night.

Louise Phelan (7)
Prestbury CE Primary School, Prestbury

Elephant

Big, bulgy elephant charging through the coconut trees.
Stomping fast through the warm splashing water.
Strolling peacefully in the boiling sunshine.
Plodding slowly through the wet rainforest.
Swinging its trunk in the beautiful moonlight.
Gently fanning its ears in the hot and sticky forest.
Slapping tail flicking all night.

Madeline Travers (7)
Prestbury CE Primary School, Prestbury

My Brother

My brother
My annoying brother
He's always hogging the TV
(And my mother)

He's always being a pest
He thinks he's the best
He loves to get me into trouble
(Just like all the rest)

He thinks he's so cool
We should be chucked into military school
He hates being good
And following any rules

My brother
My annoying brother
I love him like no other
My little brother.

Monique Taylor (10)
Rolls Crescent Primary School, Manchester

Autumn Is A Man And Woman

Autumn is a man shaking on trees
Autumn is a binman who picks up the leaves
Autumn is a woman who puts the taste in fruits
Autumn is a farmer who saves all the roots.

Saddam Osman (11)
Rolls Crescent Primary School, Manchester

Mum

She's got money,
Very funny,
Cuddle bunny,
Cooks rice with spice,
Very nice,
No tea, just like me,
(Well sometimes).
Animal lover (except for flies!)
Chocolate spy,
Chocoholic,
Shopoholic.
Got a fever,
Dancing diva
(Or so she thinks!)
She's a shiny sheen,
Clean machine,
'No stain' mad,
Not that bad.
She's my mum!

Mallisha Sinclair (10)
Rolls Crescent Primary School, Manchester

My Cousin, Poppy

She's a big time sleeper,
A cleaner meaner,
A moany sweeper,
Brave as a tiger.

She's as cute as a pussycat
But as mean as a tiger,
Skinny as a twig,
Quite tall,
Pretty as a poppy,
That's my cousin, Poppy.

Tobias Simms (10)
Rolls Crescent Primary School, Manchester

My Cousin, Shallon

Shallon the pest
Shallon nowhere near the best
Shallon the pain
He's such a strain.

He's my weird,
Annoying,
Unbearable
Cousin, Shallon.

His brain is air
And he acts like he's Tony Blair
But he does not fool me.

He's my paranoid,
Not so nice
Cousin, Shallon!

Khaleal Coleman (10)
Rolls Crescent Primary School, Manchester

The Bird In The Tree

The bird was eating a stick and leaves
Then the tree was turning pink and yellow.
The bird was sitting in the tree.
The branches are brown.
The tree and the leaves were green.

Natasha Gledhill-Bell (7)
Rolls Crescent Primary School, Manchester

Dragons And Monsters

Dragons and monsters all around.
I even get scared when they make a sound.
Roaring and roaring all day long
And it sounds like they are making a song.
Witches and wizards making spells
And turning people into dragons as well.
Now it's time to say to the dragons not to be bad or get mad.
When I say this poem you will not forget
These are the nicest dragons I've ever met.
It's time for me to go now,
I will catch you later somehow.

Taneita Taylor (7)
Rolls Crescent Primary School, Manchester

The Autumn Tree Ninja

Autumn is a green and brown ninja jumping from tree to tree
When he jumps down and lands on his feet it impresses me.
He runs like the wind with a clash of his sword
He runs, he breaks the brown leaves
And then he steals the fruit and veg,
And then he runs away, jumping over the hedge . . .

Lewis Lavery (10)
Rolls Crescent Primary School, Manchester

Mrs Autumn

Autumn is a woman, mischievous and old,
She likes to shake the trees a lot, never doing as she's told,
Autumn is a woman, washing her coloured hair,
Crunchy, crispy, crowding leaves almost everywhere.

Naomi Rumley (10)
Rolls Crescent Primary School, Manchester

My Sister

My sister, I love her to bits
And she hugs and kisses me,
Plays with me, talks to me (well possibly),
Makes me happy.
Sometimes I have to change her nappy,
That drives me crazy.

Jerome Raymond (11)
Rolls Crescent Primary School, Manchester

My Auntie

She was like a sweet,
Everyone knew her.
Nobody could put her down,
She deserved a crown!
I miss her so much,
My family still remember her
But that's not enough,
Because I wish she was here.

She never frowned,
Instead she always had a smile,
I never heard her shout
But I heard her cheesy laugh!
She never was a pest,
But she was the best!

Mohamed Elbadawi (10)
Rolls Crescent Primary School, Manchester

Autumn Lady

Autumn is a lady painting the leaves brown
With a very sad frown.

The twisting and twirling leaves
Slowly fall down.

The shaking hands of the tree
Scattering the leaves, cluttering and rattling.

The leaves fall down and make a clatter
As if they are a strong shutter.

Autumn is a lady with a brown and yellow bed!

Autumn strikes again.

Imran Pardes (10)
Rolls Crescent Primary School, Manchester

My Mum

My mum is a calendar that reminds me every day
She doesn't scream or shout at me
Whatever the consequences say.

My mum is an open door to hear what I say
She sorts out my problems in a thoughtful way.

My mum is smart and has a strong heart
She likes to drink tea with a jam tart.

My mum knows the right path to take
And knows the right decision to make.

That's my mum.

Errol Dias (11)
Rolls Crescent Primary School, Manchester

My Cousin, Darren

Cousin Darren,
He's a . . .

Army animal
Feisty mammal

Water drinker
Big eye winker

Party pooper
Sadness scooper

Eating machine
Wearing green.

Elliot Gillett (11)
Rolls Crescent Primary School, Manchester

Autumn Army

Autumn is a powerful army
crushing all the trees.
The army is like a tornado
blowing away the leaves.
Autumn is an empire
trying to take over the world.
Blowing every country's ground,
it leaves our Earth all curled.

Alia Rumley (10)
Rolls Crescent Primary School, Manchester

Hallowe'en

Hallowe'en is here again,
With bats and cats and big black hats,
With flying witches on their brooms,
They cast a spell to make kids smell,
Monsters and ghouls, they knock on your door,
'Trick or treat?' I give them sweets.

Kasha Thomas (8)
Rolls Crescent Primary School, Manchester

All About Rueben McKenzie

My brother's called Rueben McKenzie
He gets us all in a frenzy
He pulls my hair
And tickles my tum
So I have to go and tell my mum.

Mummy says don't,
But I say he won't listen to what she's saying.

Then Daddy jumps up and says,
'Shut up, Rueben is only playing!'

Phoebe Depasois (8)
Rolls Crescent Primary School, Manchester

My Mum

My mum is beautiful
My mum is sweet
She tucks me in bed
As I go to sleep.

My mum wakes me up in the morning
To get ready for school
She gives me Coco Pops
And a big fat spoon.

Serrage Osman (8)
Rolls Crescent Primary School, Manchester

Candy

Candy is yummy
Although it doesn't fill your tummy
Candy is sweet
It's my favourite treat
Candy comes in different colours, shapes and sizes
When you put it in your mouth
It's full of tasty surprises
Candy is so sugary and sweet
But please remember to brush your teeth!

Idrise Mohamed (9)
Rolls Crescent Primary School, Manchester

The Boy Who Was Sad

There once was a boy,
Who lost his favourite toy.

He was very upset,
He treated it like a pet.

He hunted everywhere,
For his teddy bear.

It was quite sad,
For that little lad,

To find the dog,
Had put it in the bog.

Leon Gledhill (8)
Rolls Crescent Primary School, Manchester

The River

When a river is born it cries
And it cries like a baby.
It swirls and curls around,
Rocks just like a whirlpool
And soon it is sliding down the mountain
Where it was born.
As it grows older it gets steeper and deeper.
As it swirls and curls
It makes whirlpools and meanders
And as it rains it makes flood plains.
I admire the river as it makes rapids
Bubbling over rocks and sprinkling sand.

In its old age it dies away,
Day by day it gets closer to the sea
Until it comes to a delta.
The river's baby days are no more.

Cameron Wrycroft (8)
St Joseph's Catholic Primary School, Frizington

My Box Of Wishes

My box of wishes is green and blue
Near my bedside it is covered in jewels
When you open it you will see gleams of light.
There's a button you should press.
Inside there's chocolate and gold
Two of the loveliest things in the world.

Demi Morley (10)
St Joseph's Catholic Primary School, Frizington

River, River

Young
The river was born in a foggy boggy bog
Which moved out in the forest
It swirled and whirled around the trees
The leaves got blown down by the breeze
They fell down in the river
Where it was steep and deep
When it tumbled down the waterfall
Listen and you would hear it roar like a tiger.

Middle
The river wandered down the slope
Then it started to flood
People went down the river in boats
When it rained the flood plain started
When it stopped it would go down low.

Old
It is old, the days have gone
The river is all alone
It will die on its own
The trees will fall
And that will be all
For this old river.

Rebecca Pugh (10)
St Joseph's Catholic Primary School, Frizington

My Box Of Wishes

In my box is a load of things,
Stored on my bed with gleaming things,
It glows at night to make me warm,
A nice silk 'S' on top,
With lots of jewels and diamonds on,
It gives me a lovely feeling every night,
It has lots of lovely dreams
And the same happens again each night.

Shannon Wincott (10)
St Joseph's Catholic Primary School, Frizington

Look At The River

Look at that river swirling and twirling.
Look at that river smashing and crashing.
Look at that river lazy and crazy.
Look at that river swirly and curly.
Look at that river rushing and crushing.
Look at that river lashing and slashing.
Look at that river sliding and gliding.
Look at that river roaring and soaring.
Look at that river funny and runny.
Look at that river cold and bold.
Look at that river muddy and floody.
Look at that river bubbly and jubbly.
Well! Just look at that river.

Courtney Wood (9)
St Joseph's Catholic Primary School, Frizington

Rivers

Young
The river is born among the mountain tops
It twirls and whirls down the valley
Streams bubble and dance to join it
Then it grows older and is no longer a baby

Middle
It starts to grow faster and faster
Zooming down the waterfalls
And crashing and dashing over the huge rocks
It meanders and swirls and twirls
It gets deeper and wider
Then it starts to grow old.

Old age
It starts to grow old and starts to slow down
Getting further to the ocean
And when it is about to leave it says goodbye.

Bethany Hughes (10)
St Joseph's Catholic Primary School, Frizington

River Poem

Young
In a mountain a river is formed
It swirls and twirls around rock pools
It splashes and dashes over the twinkly rocks
Rocks are caught and mashed and crashed
It dives down into a crashing waterfall
It cries and whines like a little baby

Middle
It curls around, meanders
It is like a tiger roaring
It gets deeper and steeper

Old
When it starts to get older it floods forming a flood plain
It soaks up all the roots and it helps the trees grow
And boats float on it
And fish are caught by fishermen.

Stuart Anderson (10)
St Joseph's Catholic Primary School, Frizington

A River

A river is born in the hills
It rushes and rushes like a bus
It tugs and hugs like a family
It jumps and jumps sprinkling like some salt
It flies and glides over a waterfall like a roller coaster

The river gets faster like a racing car
It twirls and whirls around meanders
It crashes and pushes the rocks on its bed
It forms a flood plain from heavy rain
And lush grass for grazing cows

Slowing down as it reaches the sea
Making a delta, depositing sand
Getting closer to the sea, getting older and older

Its life is over as it joins the great grey sea.

Jack Haddon (8)
St Joseph's Catholic Primary School, Frizington

The River Is Born

It clashes and mashes over the rocks.
It roars like a bear when it says its prayers.
It hits the side of the mountains
When it's really, really angry.
It erodes the big rocks when it's flowing by.

The river clashes and splashes under the bridge.
It swerves and curves when the canoes race by,
But when it gets old it stops being rough.

Lewis McDonald (9)
St Joseph's Catholic Primary School, Frizington

River

Young
The river is born in the snow
The river flies past the rocks and twirls and curls
The river cries and flies over the rocks
The river goes past the mountain like a rocket
The river splashes and crashes against its bank.

Middle
The river goes up and down the waterfall
The river goes round the meander very fast
The river floods in heavy rains
The river gets deeper and wider
And forms a grassy flood plain.

Old age
It flows through the estuary
And goes out to the ocean.

David Philip (8)
St Joseph's Catholic Primary School, Frizington

Rivers

The river is born in the high mountain peaks.
Then it sprinkles and twinkles down the hillside.
It crashes and bashes its bank.
It rushes and brushes down waterfalls.
It creeps and leaps over rocks.
It slaps and claps its banks.
It whirls and twirls around meanders.
It flows and glows through the night.
It starts steaming and screaming for rain.
It starts to flood in stormy weather
And destroys many houses.
When it reaches the sea it washes everything out.

Kieran Larkin (9)
St Joseph's Catholic Primary School, Frizington

The River

Young
The river is born on the morn, swishing, curling
It swishes, twirls through the rock
Like horses, dancing in a row.

Middle
Look at the river floating by
It looks like horses running by
Shiny and smooth in the moonlight.

Old age
Look at the river pouring out
Fish swimming, diving, flying, jumping in its current.

Bethany Byers (10)
St Joseph's Catholic Primary School, Frizington

The Playground

When the school bell rings at half-past ten
We walk out smartly on the yard
And shout, 'It's time to play!'
Children running about doing handshakes
And playing football.
People chasing each other
And running on the pitch having fun together.
The hot sun beating down on them
Then the whistle loud and deafening.

Chloe Farley (8)
Vane Road Primary School, Newton Aycliffe

A Funny Fairy Tale

The first verse contains a girl,
With red shoes, jacket and hood.
Somewhere she met a hairy, grey wolf,
Oh yes, in a dark little wood.

The second contains a pig,
Who built a house of straw.
But suddenly the wolf blew it down,
So he had to go next door.

The third verse contains a princess,
Who lived in a faraway house.
Since she was rescued by the dwarves,
She was even friends with a mouse.

The fourth verse is about an egg,
Who was sitting playing on a wall.
Until he fell off and broke his leg
And couldn't be fixed at all.

The fifth verse gets a bit scary,
With a princess who was locked in a tower.
She was not there when the prince came,
Since it was the wrong time of the hour.

Heather Archer (11)
Vane Road Primary School, Newton Aycliffe

The Playground

The bell rings very loudly.
The children walk outside smartly.
Children scream and shout at the top of their voices.
See the children munch their crisps.
Hear the teacher's whistle blowing.
Children running everywhere.
Birds screeching very loudly.
Feeling hot and sweaty.

Casey Davidson (8)
Vane Road Primary School, Newton Aycliffe

Shaunie And Charlotte's Magical Box

(Inspired by 'Magic Box' by Kit Wright)

In our magical box we would put . . .
Shiny conkers so smooth to hold,
Autumn leaves so crispy and gold,
Robins singing a sweet song,
Children playing all day long.
Spiky pine cones so prickly and brown,
Lying gently on the ground.

Shaunie Mounsey & Charlotte Weldon (10)
Vane Road Primary School, Newton Aycliffe

My Children's Poem

The first verse contains a wizard,
A horrid wizard indeed.
A green, fat, sloppy blob
And a helpless lady in need.

The second verse includes
A princess locked in a tower,
A greedy red-eyed monster
And a bee trapped by flower.

The third verse is quite different
Containing a rubber snake,
A man with a green cat
And a chicken ready to bake.

The fourth verse includes a dragon
Spitting with all its might
A knight in shining armour
Waiting for a fight.

Harriet Scott (9)
Vane Road Primary School, Newton Aycliffe

Finding A Pet

If you want a friend who is loyal
Then you should get a pet
But what animal?
I bet you can't choose!

Then I will help
You find a pet.

A small, deadly lion? No!
An Indian elephant?
It might stand on you so - no!
A slippery eel? No!
Maybe . . .
A cat or dog? Yes!
If you want a pet
And are willing to let
Them annoy everyone you have ever met
You will not regret
Finding a pet.

Emma Yeo (10)
Vane Road Primary School, Newton Aycliffe

The Writers Of This Poem

(Based on 'The Writer of this Poem' by Roger McGough)

The writers of this poem,
Are as bold as knights,
Are as busy as bees,
Are as high as kites.

Are as patient as policemen,
Are as pretty as a pearl,
Are as fast as a cheetah,
Are as curly as a curl.

Are as careful as a surgeon,
Are as jumpy as a frog,
Are as wild as a bear,
Are as bright as a dog.

Are as clever as a spider,
Are as sly as a fox,
Are as cunning as a gang member,
Are as fiddly as locks.

The writers of this poem,
Never cease to amaze -
We are two in a million billion
(Or so this poem says!)

Jessica Burke & Charlotte Weldon (10)
Vane Road Primary School, Newton Aycliffe

The Playground

The leaves crackling quietly underfoot.
Dogs howling in the icy wind.
Children splashing happily.
Gingerbread . . . *mmm*
Drifting from the kitchen.

Gabrielle Welsh (8)
Vane Road Primary School, Newton Aycliffe

Our Scary And Funny Poem

The first verse contains a garden
With a cute little gnome,
And a sly black cat,
With a huge candy home.

The second verse has a dragon,
With long powerful wings.
A bat which sucks blood
And other scary things.

The third verse contains fairies,
With sparkling, glittering wands,
And little brown scary things
In the disgusting black ponds.

The fourth verse has a ghost
Which always says boo!
And a vampire with fangs
And a scary Doctor Who.

The fifth verse contains a princess,
Who has long golden hair
And an wicked, evil witch
That says, 'It isn't fair!'

Victoria Blood & Calvin Wilson (10)
Vane Road Primary School, Newton Aycliffe

Abbie And Alisha's Magic Box

(Based on 'Magic Box' by Kit Wright)

In our fantastic magic box . . .
We would put the sight of the beautiful white geese,
Flying overhead to try to find warmth.

Also, we would put in the sight of the first
Bright red leaves falling from the tall sycamore tree.

We would put the sound of robins cheeping in the large oak tree,
Whilst the wind blows wildly through the branches.

I would love to put in our magic box
The sound of a cute, small, prickly hedgehog
Scuttling in the huge pile of leaves.

I would also put in the taste of a huge piece
Of gorgeous, mouth-watering, fresh apple pie.

I would like to place in our magic box
The smell of the fresh fatty bacon being grilled
Straight out of the packet. *Mmmm!*

Alisha Chisholm (11) & Abbie Avery (10)
Vane Road Primary School, Newton Aycliffe

Five In A Big Tent

We went camping, all of us together
We enjoyed the days no matter what the weather
We played golf and football in the rain
Some people thought we were insane
We had scones, hot chocolate, soup and cake
We also went to Ullswater Lake
Camping was the best time I've ever had
But going home was painful and sad.

Georgia Ireson (9)
Vane Road Primary School, Newton Aycliffe

The Wonderful Sound Poem

The yelling of the teacher,
The screaming of the kids,
The sound of the chairs scratching,
The popping of the lids.

The scribbling of the pencils,
The marking of the board,
The old lady singing,
Or is it really a fraud!

The slurping of spaghetti,
The crunch of a chocolate bar,
The lady saying, 'Be quiet!'
As she waits at the bar.

Holly Brown (10)
Vane Road Primary School, Newton Aycliffe

Magical Memories

(Based on 'Magic Box' by Kit Wright)

Inside my golden box I would place . . .
My grandad laughing with my sister and I,
And the sound of horses galloping through a meadow,
Also I would have a friend laughing with joy.
I would love the sound of newly born birds cheeping,
I would love the smell of freshly cooked chicken,
The smell of chocolate melting in the bowl,
Also the smell of a fresh rose just cut.
I would love to see a kitten just being born,
And a puppy as well,
I would like to feel a kitten's fur coat,
And the taste of melted chocolate on my tongue.

Cassie Law & Matthew French (9)
Vane Road Primary School, Newton Aycliffe

A Rainbow

A rainbow is a coloured flame,
It warns of coming rain.
A rainbow is a beautiful sight,
All the colours shining bright.
A rainbow is a daytime light,
Never to be seen at night.

Rhian Jones (8)
Woodfall Primary School, Little Neston

My Thoughts

I came from a distant, dark and gloomy land
where only I live far down in the muddy undergrowth.
I will travel to children's heads
and play games with their minds.
I will get there on the winds of time
which will roam at the speed of sound.
It could take me seconds or it could take me centuries
I don't know but I want to.
I will take with me the ability and power of many sorcerers
around the world and treasure them with the four elements;
air, earth, fire and water.
The thoughts in my head are curing illness
and helping people and animals less fortunate than us.
I will protect them in a titanium box as wide as a mile
defended by 100 spotty, strong leopards.
I will know when my journey has ended
when the world is at peace.
In my dreams I hope that I will transform
into a normal human being again but the magic is too strong.
When I shut my eyes I want to be human again
and to play with my best human friends.

Jack Mellor (10)
Woodfall Primary School, Little Neston

Snoutter

I come from the land of Knower where all the grass is turquoise
and the birds sing and the sun never dies down.
I will travel beyond the sky into space to see the stars and the moon.
I will get there by flying on the wind and the clouds.
My journey will take me a lifetime.
I will take my magical staff with me that gives me my life.
My thoughts will be of how my journey will end.
I will protect all my secrets with all my heart
and within all my staff's power I will protect all
and I will know when I reach my journey's end
because I will see a waterfall.
Beyond the waterfall I see a stone, it is the stone of life.
In my dreams I hope for a family.
When I close my eyes I see a town
with fluttering birds and swaying trees.

Macaulay Oswald (10)
Woodfall Primary School, Little Neston

Castle

C astle on a hill,
A moat around the tower,
S tairs to a tower,
T ower next to the moat,
L ovely princess,
E ating her dinner.

Samuel Hannah (8)
Woodfall Primary School, Little Neston

Universe Of Wonders

I come from a luminous star near a raging hot sun
100 solar years from Earth.
I will travel to the ends of the galaxies
lapping multicoloured planets everywhere I go.
I will get there on the backs of magical pixies
creating new planets as we pass the cold, deserted universe.
My journey will take the life of the sun
and as long as the sea glistens blue.
I will take my thoughts, emotions, hopes and dreams
locked in a lion's pure heart.
The thoughts that are in my mind are the gentleness of an eagle
and the birth of a fresh-born star.
The magic gnomes of the furthest planet
stow my secrets in a pocket of wisdom.
I will know I have reached my journey's end
when everyone is joyful and there is peace and harmony on Earth.
In my dreams I wish that war on Earth will stop
and people are happy.
When I close my eyes I see the elation of children
and the medieval pot of gold at the end of the rainbow.

David Nevin-Jones (10)
Woodfall Primary School, Little Neston

Oreius

I came from a sun a thousand light years away that beams in time.
I will travel to a mysterious island that no one can find.
I will gallop on a rainbow that will lead me to my accommodation
that is joyful and happy.
It will take me twenty-five million years to get there,
it will be a tiring journey.
I will take the egg of a dragon on my travels with me
and keep it in a gold box.
The thoughts that are in my mind are, will peace finally come
to my land of happiness?
A great bird will protect the secrets in my mind
that no one will ever know.
I will know when my journey ends when all the hatred and evil
is gone and has disappeared from the world of happiness and joy.
In my dreams I hope all the black magic will die and leave my land
and bring love and high spirits.
When I close my eyes I see the valley of rainbow crystals
gleaming at the moon with glee.

Jordan Stuart (10)
Woodfall Primary School, Little Neston

My Best Friends

F orever friends
R eally good ideas
I deas we share
E ntertain each other when we're glum
N ever dislike each other
D islike it when we're not together
S hare with one another.

Charlotte Rigby (8)
Woodfall Primary School, Little Neston

My Bear

My bear is scary
My bear is big
My bear is jolly
My bear is fat
My bear is happy
My bear is tatty
My bear is pretty
My bear is hairy
My bear is tall
My bear is . . .
My best friend of all.

Sasha Leighton (7)
Woodfall Primary School, Little Neston

Fruit

Fruit is crunchy,
Fruit is munchy,
Fruit can grow on trees.

Orange, yellow, green and blue,
All different colours and yummy too.

Grape, banana, apple and pear,
Eat them all or even share.

Smooth, hard, spiky or bent,
Fruit is something you should not give up for lent.

Indoors, outdoors, school or home,
Fruit can be eaten with friends or alone.

Breakfast, lunch, pudding or snack,
Juiced, fresh or in a pack.

Fruit is healthy,
Fruit is good,
So eat 5 a day like we should.

Carly Melton (7)
Woodfall Primary School, Little Neston

The Tiger

He prances
He looks
He turns around
He walks a little further
He stops
He stares
This silent creature is prepared
The grass is swaying
You see his eyes
He's staring at you,
There's no surprise.

Beth Lawley (10)
Woodfall Primary School, Little Neston

Sculpture Thoughts

I come from the sun, the distance's far, far away.
I will travel to the other side of the world in a blazing hot rocket.
I will get there by the blazing hot, hot sun going through my feet.
My journey will take time and space, through the planets.
I will take the gleaming stars so bright and shining,
so they're invisible.
The thoughts in my mind are of God calling to me
on my way so quickly.
I will protect my secrets from danger and the wild beast.
I will know when my journey has ended on top of the moon
shining so bright in the night sky.
In my dreams I hope for big adventures so big that no can do.
When I close my eyes I see this big, huge, wonderful,
gleaming rainbow.

Chloe Gardiner (10)
Woodfall Primary School, Little Neston

Flash Of Lightning

I came from the land of lava that flows beyond the rocks.
I will travel to the rising of the sun where it burns.
I get there by a jet pack rocket as fast as a Ferrari.
My journey takes me faster, within a blink of an eye.
I take with me my dreams that will be everlasting.
My thoughts are that my skin melts like a slowly burning candle.
I will protect my belongings with my heart and soul.
My journey will end with a fall of the world collapsing.
I hope for freedom for all and laughter before the world ends.
I see the bright stars looking at me and I am looking back.

Callum Cruise (10)
Woodfall Primary School, Little Neston

My Sculpture Thoughts

I came from a desert beach in Australia on an enchanted island.
I will travel to the cheesy bright moon beyond the stars up so high.
I will get there by a blazing hot red ball of fire seabed below.
My journey will take quite a few months
passing hot and roasted deserts and freezing cold snow and ice.
I will take loving memories and loved ones
around cold days and even hot days too.
My thoughts are loving and kind ones
and ready to get there in a few icy cold months.
I will protect my secrets by keeping them all up in my thoughtful head
and thinking about them every minute of every day.
I will know I have reached my journey's end
because I will be up beside the stars so very bright and high.
In my dreams I hope for love and kindness
all over the whole wide world for everybody.
When I close my eyes I see my own little island
and the large place that I am now in.

Abbie Ellis (10)
Woodfall Primary School, Little Neston

My Mythical Creature

I came from a cave deep down below.
I will travel to the middle of the coldest and bluest sea.
I will get there by the whitest cloud made out of marshmallows
and gumdrops.
It will take me 10 million light years to get there.
I will take a memory of my lifetime.
The thoughts in my mind are going as fast as a racing car.
A box of gold will protect them from danger.
I will feel tapping inside my body.
In my dreams I hope to go swimming in the Menai Straits.
When I close my eyes I will see the brightest fire
that never stops burning.

Michael Smith (10)
Woodfall Primary School, Little Neston

In The Stars

I come from the mystical beyond that's in the stars
which are glistening like a candle in the sky.
I will travel to a distant planet where there is peace and harmony.
I'll jump from star to star like a bird soaring gracefully in the sky.
My journey will be longer than it takes the sun to burn out.
I will take with me a golden star that holds my heart.
I think with excitement of living in peace and harmony.
I will keep my secrets in a golden star alongside my heart.
I will know when my journey has ended
because my nightmares will cease.
In dreams I hope for my family and friends to follow me.

Wesley Osunjimi (11)
Woodfall Primary School, Little Neston

Flaming Cerberus

I came from the snowy depths of Outer Siberia.
I will travel to the burning, scalding hot heart of the sun.
I will fly through rain, sun, snow, hail, wind and thunder.
It will take the lifetimes of 50 elves to get there.
I will take a magical star from a rainbow, multicoloured.
I will be brave, I will think of when I was a baby
Cerberus in my magic egg shielding me from the outside world.
I will protect my secrets in a golden treasure chest
and throw away the key.
You will know when it's my journey's end
when I have reached the World War 50,000.
In my dreams I hope for a treasure chest full of gold, rubies,
sapphires and emeralds.
When I close my eyes I see myself getting presented
with a star by the king.

Jack Hughes (10)
Woodfall Primary School, Little Neston

Sculpture Thoughts

I come from a dim and magical place where only 4 of me are born
every year just after the black hole.
I will roam to Sano Togo, a place under the Earth.
It is as icy as a freezer.
I will travel by a magical air bus at 1,000mph.
My journey will take as long as it takes.
I will take my precious blanket of gold,
it can be as chunky as a giant or as little as a sheet of ice.
The thoughts in my mind are growing up
and realising what the world will come to.
I will perfect myself with my fiery red nose
as blazing as a microwave after it's just been used.
My journey will end when the Earth goes to tiny little pieces.
When I close my eyes I hope for peace and harmony
and a blanket made out of dreams.
My biggest dream's my family, precious and I'm never to forget it.

Lauren Smith (10)
Woodfall Primary School, Little Neston

Starlight Secrets

I have come from a place where there are gleaming stars
as cold as ice.
I will travel to a place far beneath the Earth
where it is just black with tiny fireballs zooming past.
I will get there by a magical flying bubble
made of shining crystal and gold.
My journey will take me a long 400 days to get there.
I will take with me a bright golden ray of the burning sun.
The thoughts within my mind are hoping for my dreams to come true.
The glossy and frosted stars will protect my deepest
and darkest secrets.
I will know my journey has ended when 10 new miniature planets
appear in space.
In my dreams I hope for a world of peace and quietness.
When I close my eyes I see everyone happy and enjoying their lives.

Sarah Maxwell (10)
Woodfall Primary School, Little Neston

Mystical Beasts

I come from the planet Zorb, countless universes away
where the volcanoes dominate the skyline.
I will travel to the centre of the Earth where the heat is immense.
I shall use my 100-mile wings to thrust me
through space at 7,000,000mph.
My journey will take until I reach the end of time.
I will take with me the memories of my family.
The thoughts in mind are of the end of all wars.
I will protect my secrets at the core of the sun.
I will know my journey has ended when the universe ceases to exist.
In my dreams I hope for eternal peace.
When I close my eyes I see Zorb in harmony.

Josh Cooke (10)
Woodfall Primary School, Little Neston

Happy Birthday Moon

I will give you . . .
A beautiful red flower so you can smell the Earth.
A fluffy yellow baby chick to play with.
A dark green car so you can visit the stars
And a big silver blanket with stars on
So you can sleep through the cold winter.

I will give you . . .
All the blue waters of the Earth to swim in.
A brown chocolate cake for you to enjoy on your birthday.
A big purple ball to bounce
And a big golden bear to sleep with.

Emma Halton (8)
Woodfall Primary School, Little Neston

Horses

H orses big and horses small,
O ne lesson after the next,
R iding hats on and off they go,
S addle very black, very heavy on their back.
E veryone goes home, the lights go off.
S leepy horses now go to sleep.

Beth Livesey (9)
Woodfall Primary School, Little Neston

Sculpture Thoughts

I have come from a magical place
far beyond the unbearably dark planets.
I will go and travel to a little huddle of bright, sparkling clouds
of big views of cities.
I will get there by a space scooter
zooming with trembling winds and storms.
My journey will take 1 zooming day
and 12 slow hours.
I will take with me 10 blobberen rockets
exploding in the black sky.
With my thoughts in my mind
I wish for a peaceful world.
I will protect my thoughts by snapping them,
my rocket-powered brain full of trapped secrets.
I will know when my journey has ended
when a sign pops up and says 'Land Here'.
In my dreams I hope for a peaceful world
for all to be quiet.
When I close my eyes I see a new world
getting created and it's peaceful.

Ryan Bird (10)
Woodfall Primary School, Little Neston

Sculpture Thoughts

My home is far beyond the distant horizon,
where the mighty mountains are higher than the clouds.
I will travel over the glimmering stars and planets
to the far ends of the Earth.
I will fly on the wings of an eagle
and swim on the back of a whale.
I will travel for days on end
until the 5th sun has set behind the green hills.
I will take with me my thoughts, memories and fears.
My feelings are like the stones in the sea
scattered and all over the place.
My secrets are protected in a box of flames
and guarded by fierce dragons.
The stars will fall from the sky when my journey has ended.
I hope for world peace and happiness forever.
I see the sun burning brightly in the sky
and the moon watching over us as we sleep.

Hannah Russell (11)
Woodfall Primary School, Little Neston

Leaf Dragon

I come from the sunny USA
I will go to the sun where you burn yourself
The journey will take me a witch's lifetime
I will get there on a leaf-mobile going all the way round the world
I will take a magic stick that will give me everything I want
I hide my secrets in a treasure chest with a rusty key
I will get there in my leaf-mobile
There will be a statue of a monkey made out of gold
I hope for a better life
When I close my eyes I see darkness.

Tom McIntosh (10)
Woodfall Primary School, Little Neston

My Imaginary Wonders

I came from the heart of the misty blue water down
in the beautiful sea, brightened by the blazing hot sun.
I will travel to the shiniest star on Earth and meet the others
by the glow of the shimmering moon.
I will travel across the amazing rainbow
and pick up the magical pot of gold at the end;
I will then travel by horseback to my place of wonders.
My journey will take me 100 years of freedom and happiness
and pass by like a person's childhood.
I will take thoughts and memories of happy days
along with my golden chain which carries three precious wishes.
The thoughts within my mind are about a world of love and joy
and not a world of hate like a fire spreading rapidly.
I will summon the lord of trust and willingly leave my secrets
behind me as I continue my journey.
When my journey ends the lights will touch the Earth
and all of my thoughts will come true and secrets will be realised.
In my dreams I hope to reach the end of my journey
to find all of my family and friends waiting for me.
When I close my eyes my mother comes back home
to be with me for all of eternity.

Bryony Challoner (10)
Woodfall Primary School, Little Neston

Sculpture Thoughts

I am from animal dreams, I have come travelling through space
beyond the stars.
I will be travelling to miracle dreams with made-up animals.
I will get there with my ice-cold feet running through the flaming stars.
It will take me the time it takes for the sun to go down
and the rainbow to come up.
I will bring winds and tornadoes with the raindrops falling
on my head.
My secret to keep people away is happiness
and smiles on people's faces and peace.
When people talk to me they thank me.
I wish my miracle would come true and animals have a good life
in my dreams.
I see a smiley face and with lots of people thanking me
and jumping to me.

Catherine Connolly (10)
Woodfall Primary School, Little Neston

Happy Birthday Moon

I will give you . . .
A big Aston Martin DB7 so you can speed around space
A big yellow T-shirt so you can look colourful out in the Milky Way
A massive green armchair to sit and rest on
And a silver pair of trainers so you can run around space.

I will give you . . .
A big blue swimming pool so you can swim and splash about
A gigantic purple plum so you can eat and eat and eat
And a million golden coins so you can go shopping all the time.

James Hodgson (8)
Woodfall Primary School, Little Neston

Sculpture Thoughts

From the middle of a deserted sea
with a wonderful sandy beach, I come.
I will travel somewhere way beyond the shining sky
where no one else can get to.
My travels will take as long as it takes
for the sun and its flaming arms to go round once.
I will travel there by a magical rainbow
which I will be able to walk on to my destination.
With me; my amazing thoughts and memories of my past
and what I think will happen in the future.
The thoughts within my mind are all the wonderful thoughts
of things I will do there.
I will protect my amazing secrets that I carry with me
locked in my mind.
When I have finished my journey I will know
because all of the beautiful things I have seen will be in my mind
and my magical rainbow will end.
In my dreams I hope that something amazing like this
will happen again because it was a magical experience.
When my eyes close I see a wonderful island
above the shining sky which I once went to.

Katie Sherlock (10)
Woodfall Primary School, Little Neston

Sculpture Thoughts

I came from China where the sun is gleaming as hot as fire.
When I close my eyes I see my mum and dad lying there
on a patch of grass.
I will take the stars of the world forever.
My journey will take as long as space grows.
I will get there by swinging on vines in the green jungle.
I will travel to the end of the rainbow where there's a pot of gold.
In my dreams I hope for the planet's growth.
I will keep my secrets like a clenched fist in my mind.
The thought in my mind is the memory of space.
I will know when my journey comes to an end when my life
will be over.

Jack Ellison (10)
Woodfall Primary School, Little Neston

Sculpture Thoughts

On giant blue gas lands near the edge of the universe,
is where I come from.
I will travel to children's minds, picking up knowledge as I go.
I will turn into creatures which dive and weave
through stars and skies to get to their minds.
When the deep black universe collapses on itself
my journey will end.
I will bring magical beams from a fairy-tale trader.
The giant orcs on shooting stars make me feel frightened.
My secrets will be protected by a golden eagle swooping at enemies.
I will know when there's just white that my journey has ended.
I dream for happiness and hope through the galaxy.
When I close my eyes I see a loving and caring world.

Gary Comish (11)
Woodfall Primary School, Little Neston

Sculpture Thoughts

I came from a star called Zompithos
where everywhere is as icy and cold as Antarctica.
I will travel to a place where my creatures
will live in a roasting, murky land.
I will get there by the wind blowing me
through the stars and sun.
My journey will take me as far as the wind will take me.
I will take with me the sound of a chair scraping across the floor.
The thoughts in my mind are about the exciting journey
through the stars.
I will keep my secrets in a box in my heart that no one can get into.
I will know when I have reached my journey's end
because my heart will feel like fire.
In my dreams I hope that there will be a golden door
and when I open it, there will be a world of peace.
When I close my eyes I see a rainbow
with a door into God's magic kingdom.

Lucy Mothersdale (10)
Woodfall Primary School, Little Neston

Sculpture Thoughts

From inside the clouds I come from,
Where there are all sorts of mythical creatures.
A place where there is peace and happiness I will travel to.
My colourful sparkling wings I will travel there by.
To travel through magical winds,
It will take me three long hours.
The laughter of children, I will take with me,
In a special box that only I can open.
In my mind, my thoughts are of making happiness
Take over all evil.
With the wink of my eye, I will protect my secrets
In my golden pocket.
I will know when I have reached my journey's end
Because I will see eagles flying above me
Carrying a shining red heart to the land I am going to.
I hope in my dreams, for everyone to be happy and kind
And to help each other.
I see the world at peace and everybody helping each other,
When I close my eyes.

Natasha Jervis (10)
Woodfall Primary School, Little Neston

Sculpture Thoughts

I come from an Atlantic space club in a supersonic dark open.
I travelled with my supersonic flowers that God made.
My journey will take forever through God's golden sunshine.
I will take my sonic toad from a slimy river.
I will bring my sticky, slimy bear on my journey.
I feel so emotional so God will let it rain over me.
I will know when God lets it rain
Because there will be a rumble of thunder.
I wish I had my own intergalactic space shuttle
When I close my eyes I will see a space kid.

Simon Randles (10)
Woodfall Primary School, Little Neston

Sculpture Thoughts

My home is on the hottest burning plains in Africa
with the wonderful sands of time at my feet.
I will travel to the crumbly centre of the Earth,
surrounded by all the wriggling worms underneath it.
On the drowning rocks in the shimmering sea, I will travel.
My journey will take me as long as a tree lives,
maybe 500 times longer.
Love, peace and harmony is what I will take with me.
The only thoughts in my mind are to return to my fantastic family,
to bring more peace to the land.
To protect my secrets, the blazing sun beams down on them
and keeps them safe in his arms.
I will know when my journey's ended
when the sky lights up as blue as the sea in the morning.
In my dreams, I hope for a peaceful planet with no wars or fighting.
When I close my eyes, I am jumping over countries
to reach my family to live again.

Abbi Leighton (10)
Woodfall Primary School, Little Neston

Sculpture Thoughts (In My Mind)

I come from the sky, a place where the people can fly
and the shiny sun is as cold as ice.
I will travel to the brilliant stars in space
with my family where everybody will be happy.
I will get in a big airplane, looking at the calm blue sea
and enormous mountains tipped with snow.
My journey will take years and years,
as long as a snake.
I will take with me, the poor boys and girls and my family to be happy.
The thoughts in my mind are the poor girls and boys and my family.
I will protect my secret in the angel's heart
in the bottom of the universe.
I will know when I have reached my journey's end
by seeing peace in the sky.
In my dreams I play the violin to the poor girls and boys.
When I close my eyes, I see me playing the violin
to the poor girls and boys, and after, happiness.

Elisa Gutiérrez Moreno (10)
Woodfall Primary School, Little Neston

Sculpture Thoughts

I come from a mysterious land,
up in the clouds at the top of the Earth
where the sun gleams brightly.
I will travel to a place far beyond all the planets
and miles from the Earth.
I will get there with a magic power which nobody will use
and bounce on that sparkle in the moonlight.
My journey will take a million years
and take up part of my life which is special to me.
I will take with me my magical power
to form anything into food or water.
My thoughts in my mind I will take
will be my adventures in the past and future.
I protect my secrets by putting them in a magic box
and throwing away the key.
I will know when I have reached my journey's end
because the world will come to a new door
which will open to the future.
In my dreams I will hope for a happy start
for everyone in the land.

Emma Gillam (10)
Woodfall Primary School, Little Neston

Sculpture Thoughts

I came from a mythical island nobody has dared to come to.
I will travel further than any living creature
to a distant planet not yet discovered
in the darkest, furthest corner of the galaxy.
The fluffy clouds will take me to all the corners of the galaxy.
My journey will take me many months to cross every star and planet
to restore peace to the galaxy.
I will take the flames of the phoenix burning in my right pocket
and I will take the droplets of water from a sea serpent's tooth.
I am feeling the thought of terror and dread,
this is what will happen if I do not succeed in my mission.
The secrets of my life are inside the sun's core guarded by fire.
I will know when journey's end is here
when the oceans of distant planets shine brighter.
I hope for no wars, ruining and destroying lives and planets.
When I close my eyes I see a peaceful universe.

Nathan Fleetwood (10)
Woodfall Primary School, Little Neston

Sculpture Thoughts

I came from deep beneath the glittering sea,
somewhere I can't be seen.
I will travel to the hot, blazing sun
to show everybody that life matters.
My wings will carry me and help me travel through the blue sky.
My journey will take many centuries
for I don't know where it will end.
Many memories of happy thoughts
and a rock of the Earth I will take on my journey.
I have many thoughts in my mind
but they can never be revealed.
My secrets will be kept in a miniature box
buried underneath the ground
and I will carry a glowing key around my neck.
I will know when my journey's ended
when there is peace in the world.
In my dreams I hope for no one to be hurt or sad.
I close my eyes and I see a world that's happy
and glowing stars.

Abby Sumner (10)
Woodfall Primary School, Little Neston

The Ghost

There's a ghost under my bed,
The thing that scares me the most
Is the thought that he's dead,
He scares me at night,
It's a really big fright.

Morgan Littler (8)
Woodfall Primary School, Little Neston

There Are Two Kinds Of Worlds For Me

When I close my eyes I think of the world I am in
But in the same world there is dancing,
With the butterflies everywhere
And the rivers running through the valleys and the mountains,
It is beautiful to see birds and bees working together
To make honey and nests,
I really can't decide which world I like best
Cos there are two kinds of worlds for me.

Ashleigh Hulmston (8)
Woodfall Primary School, Little Neston

Happy Birthday Moon

I will give you . . .
A big red globe so you can search the Earth
A huge piece of yellow, delicious cake so you can eat away
A big green flower to brighten up the moon
And a shiny silver locket to wear on your birthday.

I will give you . . .
A big blue watery swimming pool so you can swim all day
A huge brown horse for you to ride on wildly
A bunch of the juiciest grapes to make a juice drink
And a glittering golden shield to protect you from meteors.

Harry Almond (8)
Woodfall Primary School, Little Neston

Happy Birthday Moon

I will give you . . .
A big juicy red apple so you can taste the fruit of Earth,
A yellow sports car so you can drive around space,
A big green, super-fast plane to go and visit your friends
And some big silver coins to spend on a bunch of flowers.

I will give you . . .
A blue Everton shirt so you can wear it,
A big brown bed to lie on and sleep on,
A big purple berry to eat on your birthday
And a golden fish scale to wear and keep you warm.

Charlie Woodhouse (8)
Woodfall Primary School, Little Neston

Happy Birthday Moon

I will give you . . .
A fat red sports car so you can drive around in it
A big yellow sun to be your friend
Some grass to smell the freshness
And some silver stars to glimmer on you.

I will give you . . .
A big massive blue Manchester United shirt
So you can wear it
A brown leprechaun
A purple berry, too juicy
Oh, and a golden necklace.

Jack Lloyd (8)
Woodfall Primary School, Little Neston

Happy Birthday Moon

I will give you . . .
A big red jacuzzi for you to bathe in
A yellow sports car for you to drive around in space
A green PS2 for you to play on
A big silver necklace to wear.

I will give you . . .
A big piece of blue sea to split your land up
A big brown bed so you can sleep in it
And a big golden bird for you to have as a pet.

James Mackenzie (8)
Woodfall Primary School, Little Neston

Happy Birthday Moon

I will give you . . .
A nice red book so you can read about the Earth.
A big yellow pen so you can write with it.
Some green grass so you can smell our lovely green earth.

I will give you . . .
A bright silver coin so you can go to the spaceport in Liverpool.
A lovely blue pool so you can play in it.
And a golden Elvis guitar so you can play on it.

Lauren Arnison (8)
Woodfall Primary School, Little Neston

Happy Birthday Moon

I will give you . . .
A shiny red jumper so you can keep warm
A yellow book so you can read at night
A green plant so you can smell the earth
And a silver coin to buy something fresh.

I will give you . . .
A big blue balloon to make you happy
A brown map to have an adventure
A purple teddy to make you happy when you are sad
And a golden beret to make you shine.

Kate Williams (8)
Woodfall Primary School, Little Neston

The Night Of Trick Or Treat

Once again it's time to shop
For fangs and blood and old black cloth
To paint your face and act the fool
In an old black sheet you become a ghoul
With bones that glow and masks that scare
You step outside in the evening air
Mum's right there but out of sight
Roaming the streets with a pumpkin light
You knock on doors with a nervous smile
Then knock again and wait a while
As the door opens up and lights the street
The kid's scared voice says, 'Trick or treat.'

Mollie Hilton-Jones (9)
Woodfall Primary School, Little Neston

Sculpture Thoughts

I come from inside a door opened from the heart of a rainbow
to a land where a mirror stands to tell the future.
That is where I will travel to.
I will reach my destination by lifting my hopes and following my heart.
My journey will take until every spark of magic
from my horn has broken off.
On my journey I will take the memory of laughter
and the lava from above the sun but below the stars.
All good thoughts within my mind are dying, for the first star of
hope has fallen.
I will protect my secrets by keeping a phoenix feather
close to my heart.
I will die when my journey has ended
and my ashes will show anyone can succeed.
When I close my eyes I see the northern lights
filled with joy to tell all bad has gone.

Hannah Wynne (10)
Woodfall Primary School, Little Neston

Monster Bed

Monsters big, monsters small
Monsters short, monsters tall
But monsters blue and monsters red
I don't like them under my bed.

Monsters funny and monsters fluffy
Monsters smelling of sweet honey
These are the monsters I like best
They can hide under my bed!

George Mellor (8)
Woodfall Primary School, Little Neston

In The Park

In the park I saw . . .
Ducks quacking loudly
Dogs running quickly
Birds flying happily
Rabbits hopping bouncily.

Grown-ups sitting noisily
Children playing joyfully
Sun shining brightly
Trees swaying gently.

Sian Cullen (9)
Woodfall Primary School, Little Neston

Silence

The alarm clock goes off,
The kettle starts to boil,
The traffic starts to stop
And the roadworks banging,
Bang, bang, bang!

Children laughing merrily,
Typing on the computer,
The ticking of the clock,
As it slowly goes round,
Tick-tock, tick-tock.

The music from next door,
The black TV is talking,
The munching of the biscuits
And the buzzing of the bees,
Buzz . . . buzz . . . buzz.

The pouring of the rain,
The banging of the thunder,
All these sounds stored in a box
And never heard again,
Silence, silence, silence.

Victoria Greenhalf (9)
Woodfall Primary School, Little Neston

Happy Birthday Moon

I will give you . . .
A big red balloon so you can have fun on your birthday,
A big yellow toy sun so you can play,
A little pair of green socks so your feet will be warm
And a silver ring so you look pretty on your birthday.

I will give you . . .
A swimming pool so you can practise your swimming,
A brown dog to play with,
A purple watch so you can tell the time
And a multicoloured rainbow to brighten up your day.

Jordyn Smitton-Cross (8)
Woodfall Primary School, Little Neston

Happy Birthday Moon

I will give you . . .
a big red juicy apple,
some yellow paint to look like your friend the sun,
the green African plain for you to play on
and a silverback male ape for you to play with.

I will give you . . .
a big blue, delicious plum for you to eat,
some brown pictures by Picasso for your bedroom to decorate it,
a purple video game so you don't get bored
and a multicoloured sports car
to make you go round the world in double-quick time.

Oliver Thomas (8)
Woodfall Primary School, Little Neston

Happy Birthday Moon

I will give you . . .
a big red balloon so you can float around in space,
a yellow, happy friend the sun, because he will keep you happy,
a green, warm blanket to keep you warm through the night
and a glittering silver sports car so you can visit all your friends.

I will give you . . .
a great blue light so you don't get scared,
a nice brown bar of chocolate so you won't get hungry,
a purple juicy grape so you can stay healthy
and a big golden mansion to live in.

Rhiannon Owens (8)
Woodfall Primary School, Little Neston

Happy Birthday Moon

I will give you . . .
a great red plane so you can fly your way round space
a lovely yellow banana so you can taste the food of the Earth
a nice green cover to sleep comfortably
and a sparkly silver set of stars.

I will give you . . .
a little blue book to read
a brown old dog to play with
a purple-stringed guitar to tune up
and a lot of multicoloured rainbows to make you smile.

Joe McKenna (8)
Woodfall Primary School, Little Neston

My Dog Alfie

My dog Alfie likes to chew on a ball
He loves hopping through long grass
He makes a racket in the hall
Sometimes I think he's really first class.

Molly-Rose Bryson (7)
Woodfall Primary School, Little Neston

Sculpture Thoughts

I came from a secret place far
beyond the flickering sun where the angels dance.
I will travel to a place where the dreadful past lies.
I will travel on my white feathery wings
that glide through the winter air.
I will travel until I hear a sound of a child screaming.
A dark memory of the darkest past I will take with me.
The thought that's in my mind is a child crying as her dad walks past.
A spider protects my hidden secrets in its sticky web.
I will know I have reached the end
when I see an innocent child smile.
I hope for a better world where the sun is beaming
on the summer sky.
I see the moon smiling and the stars dancing for joy.

Lucy Reid (10)
Woodfall Primary School, Little Neston

Sculpture Thoughts

I came from the mythical lands of the deep
Where the scorching lava flows through the misty mountains.
I will travel to the boundaries of time
where our life conducts as the world goes by.
I will glide swiftly on the mighty seven seas
as soft as burning meteorites.
My journey will take as long as there are sparkling stars in the skies.
I will take the fiery red ruby of the gleaming sun
in a case of dark imagination.
I will protect my secrets with the glowing colours of the four moons.
I know when my journey has come to an end
because the stars shine red and green with destruction.
In my dreams I hope for peace and harmony across the lands.
When I close my eyes I see hatred and suffering in the distance.

Tommy Ashbrook (10)
Woodfall Primary School, Little Neston